WAY OF THE JUNGLEPRENEUR

WORKBOOK

WAY OF THE JUNGLEPRENEUR

WORKBOOK

Junglepreneur Exercises for Succeeding and Surviving

DAVID OLUDOTUN FASANYA

CEDAR
FORGE

For permission requests, please address
Cedar Forge Press
7300 West Joy Road
Dexter, Michigan 48130

Published 2014 by Cedar Forge Press
Printed in the United States of America

18 17 16 15 14   1 2 3 4 5

ISBN 978-1-936672-79-0

Library of Congress Control Number: 2014952801

I dedicate this book to God, my wonderful family, and friends.

Note to Readers

This publication contains the opinions, ideas and philosophy of the author. It is intended to educate and provide helpful and informative material on the subjects addressed. Since each factual situation is different, the suggestions, frameworks and strategies outlined in this book may not be suitable for every individual. They are therefore not guaranteed or warranted to produce any particular results. This book is sold with the understanding that the information is not intended to render legal, financial, accounting or other professional advice or services to the reader. Before adopting any of the suggestions in this book or drawing inferences from this book the reader should consult his or her own advisor concerning that individual's specific circumstances.

The author has taken precautions in the preparation of this book and believes that the facts presented in the book are accurate as of the date it was written, but no warranty is made with respect to the accuracy or completeness of the information or references contained herein, and neither the author, nor the publisher assumes any fault for any errors or omissions. Both the author and the publisher specifically disclaim any responsibility for any liability, loss, risk, personal or otherwise, which is incurred as a consequence, directly or indirectly, of the use and application of any of the contents of this book.

Contents

Introduction

Welcome to the Junglepreneur workbook. It contains more details about the roadmap you need for achieving your dreams and thriving in any business terrain. The roadmap is the concept of Junglepreneurship, which teaches you how to tackle any business environment, overcome challenges, maximize opportunities, and use them to succeed. Before using this workbook, it is assumed that you have read the book, *Way of the Junglepreneur*, as it helps you flow into the exercises immediately. If however you have not yet read *Way of the Junglepreneur*, you can still start your Junglepreneurship journey here as this workbook contains a brief summary at the beginning of each chapter which will give you an overview of the key concepts. Nonetheless, to compliment this workbook, you are encouraged to still get your copy of *Way of the Junglepreneur* as soon as you can. This can be done through the website www.junglepreneur.com. In using this workbook, you will find out that it includes detailed exercises that guide you in deploying the exciting Junglepreneurship roadmap to become the ultimate tough-terrain businessperson, the Junglepreneur. It is recommended that you diligently work through each exercise and try to implement them on a regular basis. This way, the concepts and frameworks are more effective for you and become applicable to your business situation or terrain. Junglepreneurship is a concept that has come of age and is becoming a growing movement of people in different tough terrains from all over the world. It is finally the time of the Junglepreneurs, and this workbook will help to guide you into being a Junglepreneur.

Chapter One Development Exercises
The Junglepreneur

In chapter one of the book, we learned that the most capable beings will thrive and survive economically under the new law of survival. These people are the Junglepreneurs, who can build a business in any location and ensure its legal survival by staying Creative, Adaptable, Persistent, Aware, Brave, Linked, and Energized. Thus the Junglepreneurs are Jungle CAPABLE and able to tame any business terrain to produce successful results. The 2008 global financial crises altered the business terrain, which is now tougher, with new rules, institutions, and players. Thus the massive shift in global business will require Junglepreneurship as a survival-driven process to maximize all opportunities and overcome business challenges. Junglepreneurship is also about distinctiveness, and the three distinctions of the Junglepreneur are:

1. Formation process of the Junglepreneur,

2. Capacity of the Junglepreneur to excel in rapidly changing environments, and

3. Location of the Junglepreneur in very tough business terrains.

These three distinctions have been crystallized into what is called the Junglepreneur FOCAL Point, with FO representing Formation, CA representing Capacity and L representing Location.

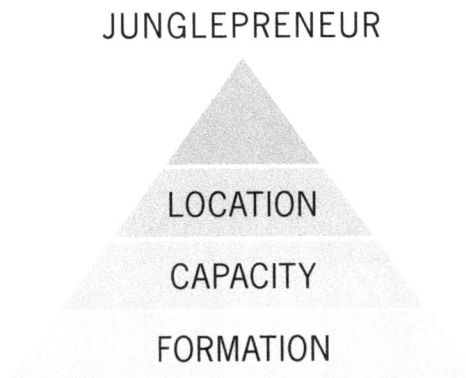

JUNGLEPRENEUR

LOCATION

CAPACITY

FORMATION

Exercises

In the following exercises, reflect on your own experiences and find your inner Junglepreneur.

1. Formation Process: Can you recall part of the experiences, knowledge, people, or places that have helped to form your traits as a businessperson? Describe these experiences and how they have shaped you.

   a. _____

   _____

   _____

   b. _____

   _____

   _____

   c. _____

   _____

   _____

   d. _____

   _____

   _____

   Now list your own top four unique traits that you believe have developed from these experiences.

   i. _____

   ii. _____

   iii. _____

   iv. _____

2. Capacity: Specify three instances in which you have excelled in chaotic, unstable, undefined, or rapidly changing business environments.

i. _____

_____

_____

ii. _____

_____

_____

iii. _____

_____

_____

List the steps, skills, or resources that you deployed to excel in these instances

i. _____

_____

_____

ii. _____

_____

_____

iii. _____

_____

_____

3. Location Adaptation: Describe briefly if and how you have been able to adapt to the business terrain you are operating in.

_____

_____

_____

_____

_____

_____

_____

_____

Now give yourself a personal score between 1 and 10, based on your level of adaptability (where 1 is lowest and 10 is highest): _____

Give examples to support your score rating:

_____

_____

_____

_____

_____

_____

_____

_____

If your score is below 6, then plan to work with a coach on improving your terrain adaptability.

4. The world of global business is evolving, and territories everywhere are experiencing a new wave of change. Try to list below any new economic or policy changes you have noticed in your territory recently in the following areas:

a. Business regulations

    i. _____

    ii. _____

    iii. _____

    iv. _____

    v. _____

b. Business institutions

    i. _____

    ii. _____

    iii. _____

    iv. _____

    v. _____

c. General business support

    i. _____

    ii. _____

    iii. _____

    iv. _____

    v. _____

Take note of the steps you took to excel and those skills or resources that you deployed. This is part of your process for excelling and will be useful as a guide for how you operate best in chaotic situations. The process you used may be replicable for achieving greater success if similar situations should require it. Also take note of the business changes going on in your environment, as the information will be useful in helping you succeed there.

Chapter One Reflections on The Junglepreneur

Note here your personal reflections from the exercises in this chapter. Also prepare a to-do list of tasks or steps you will take daily to implement the exercises.

_____

_____

_____

_____

_____

_____

_____

_____

_____

_____

_____

_____

_____

_____

_____

_____

_____

Chapter Two Development Exercises
The Business Jungle

Analogically speaking, within the central overlap of the jungle and the business world is a junglelike business terrain. This is where the essence of the Junglepreneurship concept resides. I have called this essence the Junglepreneurship CORE: Challenges, Opportunities, Resources, and Energy. The ability to overcome challenges and maximize opportunities and resources with a great amount of personal energy is what makes a businessperson succeed in any tough terrain. In the jungle you have all kinds of species: herbivores, carnivores, fruits, birds, insects, etc. It is very similar in the tough business terrains, which also have all types of players. If you look closely enough and discern based on your particular terrain, you may find in the business world actors, resources, and situations that occupy the very same roles as those in the jungle. The business jungle that the Junglepreneur operates in does not have any particular geographic location. Tough business terrains are fluid and dynamic, and they can appear gradually or suddenly. They exhibit different characteristics, which can manifest in any location and sometimes with little or no prior indication. Compared to a normal terrain, a tough business terrain has challenging circumstances present for a long time span and with major adverse effects. Challenging circumstances such as recessions, ineffective governance, or failing infrastructure can be found in the economic, governing, and socio-political aspects of a tough terrain. To survive in tough terrains, instead of thinking outside the box, discount the presence of business limitations by *thinking without the box*. Also note that tough business terrains inherently possess high levels of unfamiliarity that cannot be underestimated. Nevertheless, business and financial success is still possible in unfamiliar or chaotic business environments.

JUNGLEPRENEURSHIP CORE

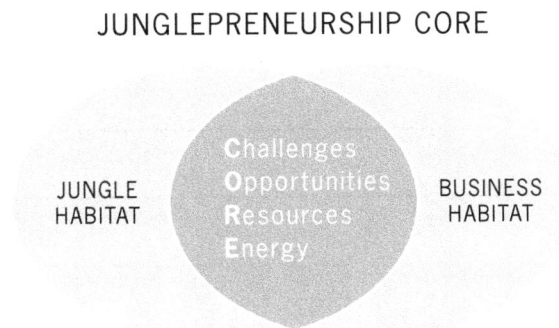

JUNGLE HABITAT — Challenges Opportunities Resources Energy — BUSINESS HABITAT

Exercises

1. Try to identify if your terrain is a tough one by listing five challenging characteristics. The book (*The Way of the Junglepreneur*) has an extensive list in a table under the section "Tough Places, Tough Times, Tough People." However, here the criteria for identifying your terrain can be the manifestation of any of the circumstances that you consider tough.

    a. _____

    b. _____

    c. _____

    d. _____

    e. _____

2. If you have been able to identify at least five characteristics, then compare it to what you would consider to be a normal terrain. If there is disparity, then there is a high chance that you are in a tough terrain. The next step is to try to attain a commitment level that will be necessary to tackle this terrain. The way to address the issue of commitment is to decide now if you want to tackle this tough terrain or not by marking one of the options below.

    ☐   Yes, I have finally decided to tackle my tough business terrain.

    ☐   No, I have decided not to tackle my tough business terrain.

3. A. If you marked *No* in the previous question, can you state below in your own handwriting why you have decided not to tackle your terrain? Keep coming back to your *No* statement after three months to see if your reasons are still valid.
    My reasons for choosing not to tackle my terrain are:

    _____

    _____

    _____

    _____

    _____

B. . If you marked Yes in the question above, then make a personal written commitment now. In your own handwriting, write your simple statement below explaining why you have decided to tackle your terrain and what you will do to ethically survive and succeed in your tough environment. Sign and date your personal statement after concluding it, and keep this page safe.

_____

_____

_____

_____

_____

_____

_____

_____

4. Now that you have committed yourself in writing to tackling your tough terrain, you can use the statement as one of your motivational tools whenever you need it. This is a first step in trying to rebuild commitment. Other steps include having a support group or a mentor who can help you with pulling through your low times while tackling a tough terrain.

5. Consider any limitation that you may presently be facing in your business situation. See the limitation as a box, and try to remove that box from your mind. Now list below at least five alternative options that you can consider if the box is not there.

a. _____

b. _____

c. _____

d. _____

e. _____

Choose from these options the one that you can implement at the least cost and with the highest level of effectiveness.

Chapter Two Reflections on
the Business Jungle and Junglepreneurship

Note here your personal reflections from the exercises in this chapter. Also prepare a to-do list of tasks or steps you will take daily to implement the exercises.

_____

_____

_____

_____

_____

_____

_____

_____

_____

_____

_____

_____

_____

_____

_____

_____

_____

Chapter Three Development Exercises
Junglepreneur MINEKIT Foundations

Become a Junglepreneur with the Junglepreneur MINEKIT, which contains specific knowledge tools and is comprised of Mindset, Innovation, Network, Energy, Knowledge, Income, and Traits. The Junglepreneur MINEKIT is supported by having direction and choosing a specific business area. This is to ensure your business ladder is not placed on the wrong wall. Concentrate on your corporate vision for the business or project by constantly having a sharp, clear, detailed picture for what you want to achieve eventually. Also use the Junglepreneur Task Tunnel, which involves concentrating on your tasks and quantifying and ranking them as the route to accomplishing your set goals. Next have a focused approach to the business jungle by congregating all your human abilities and resources into one place and direction to intently create a powerful force for achieving your goals. Then put all your personal ability, skills, talents, and intellect into doing every task with the highest quality to achieve excellence. Next engrain excellence through habit in times of leisure. Furthermore, ensure your brain constantly works at maximum capacity by giving it enough energy from eating the right foods, exercising, and getting adequate rest. Finally, reduce costly mistakes by double-checking everything for errors or omissions, and then repeat the exercise by double-checking again or getting someone else to double-check for you.

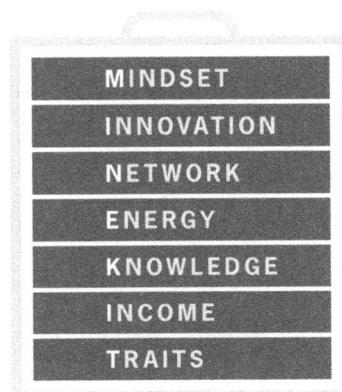

MINDSET

INNOVATION

NETWORK

ENERGY

KNOWLEDGE

INCOME

TRAITS

Exercises

1. Decide now what the vision for your business is. Have the end picture in your mind as a vivid, clear, and sharp picture, and then describe it in writing below:

_____

_____

_____

_____

_____

_____

_____

2. Practice focus now by finding a quiet place where you can concentrate for about 15 to 20 minutes. Next consider an important goal or challenge in your business terrain that you need to tackle. Then for the chosen time, concentrate all your attention on what is required to achieve the goal or solve the problem. It will be beneficial to record your thoughts in writing below, or alternatively, you can speak your thoughts out loud and record them in a voice recording. If, however, you already know what is required to achieve your goal, you should rather plan to carve out a block of time to focus on doing all the activities required without any external distractions.

_____

_____

_____

_____

_____

_____

_____

_____

3. Implement your goal-setting process by first getting a clean sheet of paper or opening a computer file to store your content. Now that they are in written format, identify the daily or weekly tasks you need to accomplish your goals. Prepare your Junglepreneur Task Tunnel and quantify the first set of tasks in terms of resources required. Then rank them based on the financial cost or physical effort they will take. List the first five tasks below:

a. _____

b. _____

c. _____

d. _____

e. _____

Then quantify the next five tasks, and again rank them below. You can decide to choose a third set of tasks at your discretion and rank those too.

a. _____

b. _____

c. _____

d. _____

e. _____

Now prepare a plan to take action on the first five tasks. Then as these are being completed, plan to start the next set, and then plan the third set if you have this. Write your full plan our below.

_____

_____

_____

_____

_____

_____

_____

_____

Finally, decide on a date and time here _____ to begin taking action on these tasks, and start at this time. Also set a completion date and time here _____ for when you will finish doing the tasks

4. Take five to 10 minutes right now to list out some additional information about your brain, based on what you already know about it. Write out information you know about its nature and the best foods, nutrition, and exercises that it requires to operate efficiently. This process will reveal if you need to get more personal information about the brain. If necessary repeat this exercise regularly, once a month. This helps you to track your knowledge and development in this area and to identify ways to maximize this key resource—the brain.

_____

_____

_____

_____

_____

_____

_____

5. Put the double-check principle into action by consciously making the effort to use the process in most activities carried out in relation to your goals and vision. List five major tasks or goals below that you will use the process for, in relation to your vision.

a. _____

b. _____

c. _____

d. _____

e. _____

Chapter Three Reflections on Junglepreneur MINEKIT

Note here your personal reflections from the exercises in this chapter. Also prepare a to-do list of tasks or steps you will take daily to implement the exercises.

_____

_____

_____

_____

_____

_____

_____

_____

_____

_____

_____

_____

_____

_____

_____

_____

_____

_____

_____

Chapter Four Development Exercises Junglepreneur Mindset and Innovation

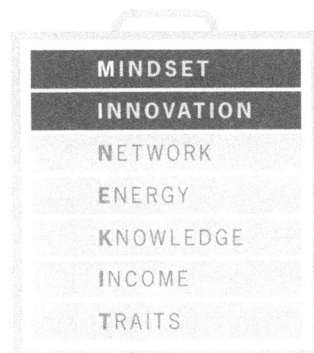

F rom the components of the Junglepreneur MINEKIT, the first two critical components are *mindset* and *innovation*. Innovation means thinking in a uniquely different way from everyone else and doing things in a special way or with an unusual twist. Mindset operates in the realm of the human brain, which is one of the most complex human organs we have. The brain is also like a computer that runs software of various kinds. Our mindset, then, is the software running in the brain.

The mindset is also the way the mind has been trained, wired, and programmed to act and react to different stimuli and situations. The mindset of the Junglepreneur is one of the most critical requirements to have success in any endeavor. It is vital that the mind runs the right software and operates the brain in the most efficient way. Achieve the right mindset by training your mind to react to different stimuli and situations in an effective manner. You also develop your mindset through reflection; thinking positive, high-quality thoughts; and by stretching your thinking capacity through brainstorming, puzzles, mind-mapping, meditation, etc.

Mindset is also built by becoming tough and developing a thick skin to challenges. You achieve this by maintaining your desire, enthusiasm, and hope in your greater future, so don't let anything or any situation keep you down. You also need to protect your mindset from negative narratives always and at all cost. So constantly ensure your mind is only running motivational narratives with the right kind of positive, encouraging, enhancing messages. Hone your mindset by taking notice and being constantly aware of what is going on in your environment and ensuring you see things with an effective perspective. Also seek the ability to achieve detached objectivity so you can see other aspects of a situation. Do this by imagining you are in a helicopter and imagining the viewpoints you can get on the situation from an elevated level. Fine-tune your mindset abilities by avoiding panic and managing your own emotions and those of others well. Then aspire to creative innovation by doing something new or reinventing something old. Also redefine current realities in light of what could be and harness or reorganize resources to create value.

Exercises

1. List ways in which you can stretch your mental capacity. You can use as examples things such as solving puzzles. Choose at least three ways to best develop your mental capacity for the next three months. List them below and commit to learning or doing them:

    a. _____

    b. _____

    c. _____

    After three months add at least another five more activities, and carry on doing all of them for the next year.

    _____

    _____

    _____

    _____

    _____

2. Every two or three hours during your workday, take out five minutes to try to recall the major narratives your mind has been playing recently. Identify the nature of the narratives, whether they are positive or negative. Try to identify the real source of where and how they came into your mind. If you are satisfied that the narratives your mind is playing will lead you to your desired vision and goals, then continue. If otherwise, start a fresh narrative that you want. This is a private game you can play every day. From this game, write out your major narratives below.

    _____

    _____

    _____

    _____

    _____

Go through the narratives you have written out and note the common thought patterns you have and what you appear to be saying to yourself on a regular basis. It should be interesting for you to see this conscious stream of your thoughts and if they are in line with your desired goals and objectives.

3. To sharpen awareness, chose one landmark that you pass by daily while commuting or that is in your home or workplace. Now try to notice three things about it you did not notice before. Or try to spot a new building or structure you did not notice before. Do this for five days, and take note of what you noticed below.

Day 1: _____

_____

Day 2: _____

_____

Day 3: _____

_____

Day 4: _____

_____

Day 5: _____

_____

4. To develop panic resistance, write out below all the possible life and business situations or scenarios that could cause you to panic if they should occur.

_____

_____

_____

_____

_____

Now read through this list once a day, and tell yourself, "I will never panic, no matter the situation." Repeat this for two to three minutes every day for a month or as long as you feel comfortable with it. What begins to happen is that the message goes into your subconscious mind, and you may be better prepared when faced with a situation.

5. In this exercise we will handle perspective, helicopter view, and emotional intelligence.

A. For emotional intelligence, at any point in time that you remember to do so, try to identify the exact emotions you are feeling and why you feel so. Also make it a habit to identify the emotions that others are displaying and why. Try this exercise out now by clearly identifying and the emotions that you are feeling right at this moment and writing them below.

_____

_____

_____

Now think through why you have these emotions. Ask yourself questions about how you got these emotions and if they are the emotions you need to reach your goals and vision.

B. For your perspective on life, describe here briefly how you see life and the world generally.

_____

_____

_____

_____

Think through what you have written. Is your life perspective or the way you see things realistic? Can it be relied upon to help you deliver results?

C. To get a helicopter viewpoint, consider a situation and imagine you were in a helicopter high above, looking down on that situation. Now try to view the situation from different angles you could not see before. Ask yourself what you could not see before, and write down four things you can now see.

1. _____

2. _____

3. _____

4. _____

Now compare what you have written down to the initial way in which you were looking at the situation, and note the differences. Consider how these differences help you to understand the situation better.

Chapter Four Reflections on Mindset and Innovation

Note here your personal reflections from the exercises in this chapter. Also prepare a to-do list of tasks or steps you will take daily to implement the exercises.

_____

_____

_____

_____

_____

_____

_____

_____

_____

_____

_____

_____

_____

_____

_____

_____

_____

_____

_____

Chapter Five Development Exercises
Network in the Jungle

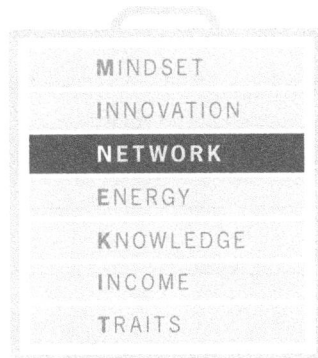

MINDSET
INNOVATION
NETWORK
ENERGY
KNOWLEDGE
INCOME
TRAITS

The *N* in the Junglepreneur MINEKIT refers to the *network* of interactions or linkages between you, other people, and the business terrain itself. So this means managing yourself, understanding others, knowing the players in the terrain, discovering what makes the terrain tick, and then being able to negotiate your way through. You are the one to fit all the parts of the network together, so let's start with you and what you need to know and have. First, the personal attributes you require for succeeding in the business jungle include being smart, savvy, aware, and tactful. Second, every terrain has features that guide the level of power and influence that is brought to bear. So the Junglepreneur must be adept at building a power base by knowing what's going on, whom to talk to, and which groups to support. Third, the Junglepreneur's access to resources, knowledge, expertise, or influence—including being trustworthy, reliable, and dependable—are all useful in the process of consolidating a network for succeeding. Start building your network by first conquering failure through learning from your mistakes, never seeing yourself as a failure, and by understanding it is all part of the success process. Develop your network by knowing the key players in your terrain, values you have in common, and your mutual benefit to each other. Understand personalities so you can relate with people, know what makes them tick, and thereby make the right judgment calls. Maximize your network by negotiating anything that requires parting with any form of value, as this is always at stake in the network. Consolidate your network by successfully managing your emotions and experiences, which are also critical in this process.

Exercises

1. Have a vision for the kind of people you need in your network, and begin to go out of your way to cultivate these relationships. Identify below the characteristics of these people.

    _____

    _____

    _____

    _____

    _____

2. Begin to identify the players in your terrain by listing the top five most influential people who are important to your success.

    a. _____

    b. _____

    c. _____

    d. _____

    e. _____

3. Write out below how you can meet these people, and understand specifically why you need to meet them.

    _____

    _____

    _____

    _____

    _____

    _____

    _____

4. Describe below what characteristics, skills, or resources you have to offer the influential people in your terrain.

_____

_____

_____

_____

_____

_____

_____

5. Choose one working week to understand personality types. First decide which personality method to use from those mentioned in the book (e.g., OCEAN Method or Hippocrates Method). Next, starting with Monday, assign one personality type to each working day of the week. Study the personality type chosen for each day very well, and list the characteristics of the personality. Try to identify people you meet that day who fit this personality. A sample log of this exercise using the Hippocrates Method is below.

Monday (Sanguine): _____

_____

Tuesday (Choleric): _____

_____

Wednesday (Melancholic): _____

_____

Thursday (Supine): _____

_____

Friday (Phelgmatic): _____

_____

Chapter Five Reflections on Network

Note here your personal reflections from the exercises in this chapter. Also prepare a to-do list of tasks or steps you will take daily to implement the exercises.

_____

_____

_____

_____

_____

_____

_____

_____

_____

_____

_____

_____

_____

_____

_____

_____

_____

_____

Chapter Six Development Exercises
Junglepreneur Energy

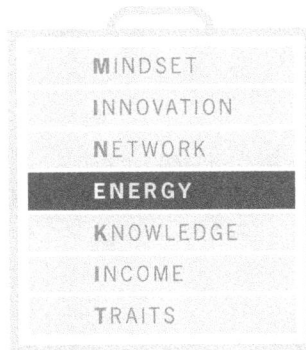

E is all about your personal *energy* and your ability to harness, preserve, and deploy it toward succeeding in your terrain. Your energy is central to all aspects of the Junglepreneur MINEKIT, Junglepreneurship CORE, and Jungle Capability. It drives all three. With the right level of energy, you can take on the challenges in your terrain and maximize all the opportunities and resources. The new law of survival emphasizes that the most capable beings will thrive and survive. However, this law too relies on energy for it to be accomplished. The Junglepreneur must always remember that for as long as it is about survival, then it is also about energy and how to manage and control it effectively. There are three aspects, which give you control of your own energy. These are generating, protecting, and deploying your energy mainly toward succeeding in your terrain.

Generate energy by starting your day with positive thoughts and affirming statements from the second you open your eyes. Be free from negativity when you wake up so you start the day energized. Boost your energy in the morning with exercise, deep breathing, breakfast, and drinking water. Maintain and replenish your energy through the day by watching your thoughts, feeding, hydration, and breathing to ensure they are in line with the good standards set in the morning. Preserve energy by avoiding energy killers, or E-Killers. These arise from situations or even relationships that can drain your energy and leave you tired, lethargic, and unproductive. Recognize manipulation and limit being manipulated so it also does not deplete your precious energy.

Allocate some time out of the first eight hours in the day to work on your goals, and maximize the undissipated energy you get from this quiet time for more productivity. Understand business herd behavior so you gain from the synergy without wasting your own energy. Have backup plans—up to Plan Z—to avoid losing energy due to correcting things that go wrong. Deploy energy by using your saved energy to create value in form of goods, services, inventions, or knowledge. Ensure mobility of all these and yourself. Furthermore, deploy your preserved energy toward networking effectively, connecting with loved ones, achieving your personal goals, communicating, and securing your physical and intellectual assets.

Exercises

1. Find positive triggers to get you started on a positive note the minute you wake up. It could be a favorite person, song, quote, thought, etc. Write out at least five of them here, and use them first thing in the morning.

   a. _____

   b. _____

   c. _____

   d. _____

   e. _____

2. E-Killers drain or take away one's energy. Identify five E-Killers that take away your own energy.

   a. _____

   b. _____

   c. _____

   d. _____

   e. _____

   Now write out a personal plan below for how to manage or avoid these E-Killers so they do not hinder your vision, goals, and objectives.

   _____

   _____

   _____

   _____

   _____

   _____

   _____

   _____

3. Although morning times may be preferable, work out the best slot during any time of the day that is an effective time for you to achieve certain objectives. Determine to take this time out, and have a plan to limit all distractions that can prevent you from maximizing this time slot. List out below the main activities, tasks, or goals that you will do during this time.

a. _____

b. _____

c. _____

d. _____

e. _____

4. If you lose assets, you will lose energy in replacing them. So be more security-conscious with your physical and intellectual assets and resources. Constantly carry out a vulnerability assessment by preparing your checklist of areas of potential weaknesses that can be exploited by others.

a. _____

b. _____

c. _____

d. _____

e. _____

Think through how you can protect these assets and write out a plan below.

_____

_____

_____

_____

_____

_____

_____

5. Identify your own five most effective means of business or personal communication, and perfect ways to utilize these to your best ability. List them below:

a. _____

b. _____

c. _____

d. _____

e. _____

Chapter Six Reflections on Energy

Note here your personal reflections from the exercises in this chapter. Also prepare a to-do list of tasks or steps you will take daily to implement the exercises.

_____

_____

_____

_____

_____

_____

_____

_____

_____

_____

_____

_____

_____

_____

_____

_____

_____

_____

Chapter Seven Development Exercises
Terrain Management Knowledge

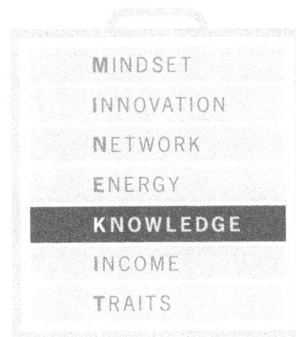

MINDSET

INNOVATION

NETWORK

ENERGY

KNOWLEDGE

INCOME

TRAITS

Acquire specific *knowledge* that is necessary for adapting to your business terrain and succeeding in it. The first three areas are knowledge about people, strategy, and systems. Learn how to manage human beings, as it is an essential requirement for your success in any terrain. You do this by understanding people, relating to them, and building teams. Get knowledge on strategy, which gives you a detailed plan for your success. It is a keystone for your business survival and for taming your terrain. Achieve understanding of the intricacies of business systems. Systems are mechanisms used to convert resource inputs into outputs in an efficient process, and they are vital to the Junglepreneur.

Manage your time by managing well the activities your time is used for. Do this by carving up your daily time by the minute and hour, and then monitor and record how each unit of your time is spent. Get a grip on complexity and turbulence, which are characteristics of tough terrains. Decompile the complex by breaking down its components into simple units. Learn to multitask, and be flexible and adaptable to the terrain.

Ensure you can identify your terrain opportunities efficiently by comparing the actual business situations to the desired situations in your terrain. Then note the gaps that have the potential to generate reasonable value and be maximized. Identify potential business risks in your terrain and the level of risks you can handle. Manage the risks by assessing them, taking steps to reduce uncertainty, and making plans to mitigate risks.

Exercises

1. Team-building skills involve team selection, vision articulation, structuring, communication, cohesion, motivation, and reward, among others. Using these, develop a core team of people you can rely on to help you achieve your vision and goals. Start by drawing up a list of five to 10 people who can form part of your team. Decide on a final team of four to six people and write out their names below. Also highlight the two to three who are the most vital to you, and ensure mutual commitment with them. Then forge your team together using the identified team-building skills.

_____

_____

_____

_____

_____

_____

2. Write out below the main points of a strategic plan for your business and terrain based on the following:
   a. Strategic analysis of your challenges, strengths, opportunities, environment, resources etc.
   b. Strategic options of frameworks and tools you can use.
   c. Strategy implementation relating to how you will measure and evaluate your strategy.

_____

_____

_____

_____

_____

_____

_____

3. Identify the type of business systems—like financial, sales, or productions systems—that you will need to succeed, and apply them to your goals or vision. Write out below the main systems that will be relevant to you.

_____

_____

_____

_____

4. In managing your activities, list five to 10 of your main daily activities below. Then work out how much time you are presently using for each core activity. Try to work on gradually reducing the time spent on each activity by 20 to 50 percent without losing efficiency. Do this over a period of time, and then start increasing your execution speed incrementally until you reach the best speed for the best results. Allocate the extra time saved to other beneficial activities.

_____

_____

_____

_____

5. Develop the capacity to recognize and maximize opportunities by allowing flexibility in assessing situations. Always look closely at what is going on around you, and consider situations from other stakeholders' perspectives, like customers or competitors. In this regard, what would the situations look like, and how would others see them? Describe this in detail below. This exercise is to try to see things from another perspective and be objective.

_____

_____

_____

_____

_____

6. A. Apply the same concept in number 5 above, to the concept of risk. Identify below the risks to your business from different perspectives.

_____

_____

_____

_____

_____

_____

B. After identifying the risks, map out a plan below for managing these risks using this risk-management process: Outline the overall goal or vision you are managing risks for. Identify all possible risk exposures. Estimate and assess the possible effects of the exposures. Evaluate the risks for embedded opportunities and threats. Mitigate these by an articulate risk-mitigation strategy. Constantly monitor all identified and potential risks. Continually assess performance and effectiveness of your risk-management process.

_____

_____

_____

_____

_____

_____

_____

_____

_____

_____

_____

_____

7. In handling complexity, consider any complex situation you have now, and try to imagine the simple components of that situation. Take a car, for example: despite its complexity, a car can be simplified to doors, an engine, a trunk, tires, seats, mirrors, etc. So use this same analogy for that complex situation, and describe some of the simpler components:

_____

_____

_____

_____

_____

_____

Now that you have listed the simple components, get a better understanding of each simple unit in terms of what makes it tick. Go through all the components, and then reconsider the complex situation, as you will likely now have a better perspective on it. Write out this new perspective below.

_____

_____

_____

_____

_____

_____

_____

_____

_____

_____

_____

Chapter Seven Reflections on Terrain Management Knowledge

Note here your personal reflections from the exercises in this chapter. Also prepare a to-do list of tasks or steps you will take daily to implement the exercises.

_____

_____

_____

_____

_____

_____

_____

_____

_____

_____

_____

_____

_____

_____

_____

_____

_____

_____

_____

Chapter Eight Development Exercises
Income in the Business Jungle

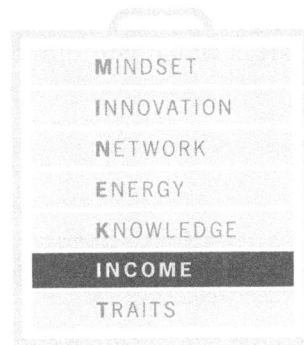

In the Junglepreneur MINEKIT, the second *I* is the *income* that you earn in your terrain. Earning your income often involves money. No matter how rough or tough the terrain is, there is money to be made all around, and it is closer than you think. Decide to get a piece of the pie by doing all it takes to make money legally. Make money by taking a closer look within your terrain to see opportunities and following where and how money flows there. Identify income streams, big spending patterns, and the market dynamics in your terrain to see how you can connect to the income streams. Connect by constructing your Junglepreneur Money Pipes, which are systems that efficiently produce and deliver your products and services of good value at the least cost to a large number of customers regularly.

Identify your skills and, with focus and courage, apply them toward the construction and implementation of your Junglepreneur Money Pipes so you maximize your income-earning potential. Go for business "big game" at least once in your career. This is a big vision or large business project that will generate large, consistent, and enduring cash flow and income for you. Have a bread-and-butter backup survival strategy that you can fall back on for short-cycle cash flows. Do this by having at least one cash-based business that brings income on a regular basis, like retail, food, or transportation. Avoid your business systems halting by making all legal efforts to keep cash constantly flowing in and out of your business in a cash-flow cycle.

Ensure you raise different kinds of capital for your business—like cash, asset, or sweat—for balance. The greatest capital, however, is you—your reputation and the confidence others have in your abilities. Make money by mastering the selling process, involving product knowledge, pricing, marketing, delivery, and post-sales service.

Exercises

1. Study your terrain, and list five income streams you can identify.

   a. _____

   b. _____

   c. _____

   d. _____

   e. _____

2. Identify and describe below some areas which you think the people in your terrain spend their money.

   _____

   _____

   _____

   _____

   _____

3. Now it is time to start working on building your Junglepreneur Money Pipes. So choose five business areas that you believe you could develop a good profitable business in. These areas could be Web-based businesses, business-to-business (B2B), retailing, service, products, or trading. Confirm the potential of your business areas by gathering transactional information about their viability. These can be obtained from trusted sources like chambers of commerce, trade associations, and established businesspeople. Now list your chosen business areas below.

   a. _____

   b. _____

   c. _____

   d. _____

   e. _____

4. Next consider these business areas from number 3 above, based on considerations like market size, costs, routes to market, location, risk, potential profit, sustainability, and social impact. Now, on a scale of 1 to 10, rank the business areas accordingly for each of the listed considerations here. Write out at least five ranked business below.

_____

_____

_____

_____

_____

Now choose your top two business areas from the ranked list of five above that you would be happy to commence operations on.

5. Next conduct your personal skills audit by identifying here the top five unique skills or talents you possess that will help drive your business.

a. _____

b. _____

c. _____

d. _____

e. _____

6. Finally, now choose the best three skills or talents from number 5 above and decide to apply them to your top one or two business areas you have ranked. This whole combination is the foundation of your Junglepreneur Money Pipe. Write out your plan to begin using these skills to operate in the chosen business area. This process as outlined commences the construction of your money pipe.

Chapter Eight Reflections on Income

Note here your personal reflections from the exercises in this chapter. Also prepare a to-do list of tasks or steps you will take daily to implement the exercises.

_____

_____

_____

_____

_____

_____

_____

_____

_____

_____

_____

_____

_____

_____

_____

_____

_____

_____

_____

Chapter Nine Development Exercises
Traits of the Junglepreneur

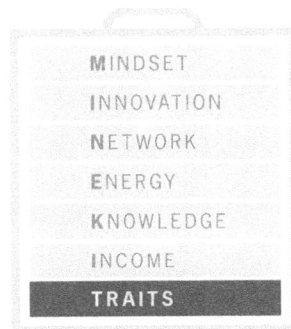

MINDSET
INNOVATION
NETWORK
ENERGY
KNOWLEDGE
INCOME
TRAITS

Your traits as a Junglepreneur are unique because upon waking up every day, these traits have to be dependable enough to enable you to survive and thrive. These traits are your Junglepreneur Person-Specific Assets (PSA), and they really are very necessary to survive the tough business jungle. In many instances, these Junglepreneurship traits have a life-and-death meaning to the economic prosperity and even the physical survival of the Junglepreneur in tough terrains.

Acquire or hone your Junglepreneur PSA to derive maximum benefit through them for each and every passing moment of every single day in the business jungle. Developing your traits requires you to utilize willpower to overcome obstacles, maximize decision making, and achieve set goals in your tough terrain. You also need to activate discipline consciously to stimulate the behavior necessary for achieving your business purpose despite basic human desires and emotions. Then exercise adaptability in your tough terrain by being flexible, pragmatic, and nimble enough to leverage every little opportunity to gain higher value. Also display competent behavior to attract people and relate well with vital allies in your terrain. Do this by caring and by conducting yourself well in speech and action.

Furthermore, hone your instinct so it serves you well as an internal warning system in your terrain. Be sensitive to internal alarm bells in business situations. If it does not feel right, then it probably is not. Gain the high stamina needed to cope with physical and mental demands of tough terrains. Exercise regularly to gain this stamina and thus avoid lethargy or ill health, which could limit your abilities for success. Also establish perseverance in your efforts by deciding to resist limitations from your environment. Commit to making one more effort continuously toward your vision, and reward yourself for this. Finally, delay personal gratification when necessary, and exercise self-control over desires, needs, and wants that are not in line with your vision. Develop the ability to maintain calmness and a level head when things get out of control by controlling your panic and fear levels.

Exercises

1. List out below your five most common personality traits that you have identified over time. If you are not certain of your common traits, you may also ask someone who knows you well to assist you with this process.

   a. _____

   b. _____

   c. _____

   d. _____

   e. _____

2. Identify your major life goals, and then consider the listed traits carefully to see if they are suitable enough to get you to your desired goals. Test the suitability of the traits by taking each trait and matching it below against all your goals to see if it helps you achieve the majority of the goals. This is called the Junglepreneur 70% Rule. That is, if a trait is not required by at least 70% of your goals, then choose another. Continue this process until you can decide on at least five good traits you need to succeed. Then consider truthfully if you already possess these traits or will need to get trained in order to acquire them.

   _____

   _____

   _____

   _____

3. Take a firm decision to persevere in all you do concerning business. Ensure perseverance by identifying a small reward or gift that can keep you motivated whenever you feel like giving up on a goal. After this, make one more effort toward your goal, and then reward yourself for this effort. Perseverance can also be built up through regular spoken affirmations that you know from experience always encourage you. You can prepare affirmative sentences, such as saying, "I will succeed no matter the obstacle," or, "I have the ability to see all my goals through." Now write out your own affirmation statement below.

   _____

   _____

_____

_____

_____

_____

4. To sharpen instinct and mental alertness, try to always determine with your sixth sense what is going on in the immediate environment around you. A good way of trying to achieve this is by quieting yourself, being calm, and tuning in more intently to sights, sounds, smells, weather, or the energy you can perceive from the environment. Practice this now for about 15 to 20 minutes and write out below what you just sensed from your environment.

_____

_____

_____

_____

_____

_____

5. To get started on physical stamina, commit to start using at least 10 to 20 minutes each day to stretch your body and do light exercises. All you need is a little start. Then build up from there. As you progress you can spend more time doing these exercises. Identify below about five exercises you can do that are suitable for you, based on your personal health and fitness circumstances. Then choose two or three exercises that you will focus on, and fix the time in the day to do them. You can find an accountability partner to help you maintain your commitment to the exercises.

_____

_____

_____

_____

Chapter Nine Reflections on Traits

Note here your personal reflections from the exercises in this chapter. Also prepare a to-do list of tasks or steps you will take daily to implement the exercises.

_____

_____

_____

_____

_____

_____

_____

_____

_____

_____

_____

_____

_____

_____

_____

_____

_____

_____

Chapter Ten Development Exercises
The Junglepreneur Attitude

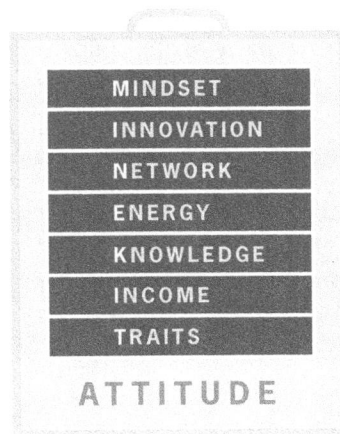

At any given time, attitudes can determine your behavior, consciously or unconsciously. Attitudes too are influenced by our ideas, beliefs, and values and developed through our learning, experiences, and emotions. Even more than ability, attitude is the key determinant of success, and it will also determine how effectively you use the Junglepreneur frameworks and the level of results you will get. Your attitude influences all your behavior and will also have an impact on how you will use the Junglepreneur MINEKIT.

Developing the right attitude starts with exhibiting courage to overcome fear and take action. Achieve this by giving no attention to fear so it does not distract you from becoming successful. Next keep your dignity, and treat others with dignity. Show poise, calmness, grace, and strength in the face of challenges. Do this by remaining stoic even if you don't feel like it. Also have confidence in your own abilities and shun negative narratives by focusing on your strengths and using your past successes as proof of what you can achieve.

Discover your true potential by carrying out an audit of your personal abilities, opportunities, and weaknesses. Then set your internal expectations at the right level, based on your actual potential and abilities. Importantly, you need to take action, and don't procrastinate. Your actions will define who you will be. Furthermore, motivate yourself to succeed by tying your motivation to emotional anchors that link to what you care about. Use your pain and success as fuel to greater heights. Finally relax, laugh, and have fun while working at your goals. Always see the brighter side of things, and enjoy the whole process of succeeding.

Exercises

1. Can you identify the type of attitude that you exhibit most of the time? A good way is to ask those around you for honest feedback about your attitude. Ask for about six to 10 traits about yourself. Classify the traits into positive and negative, and list them below.

   Positive Traits: _____

   Positive Traits: _____

   Negative Traits: _____

   Negative Traits: _____

   After the feedback, check to see how many of the traits are positive and how many are negative. If the number of positive traits is greater than the negative, then your overall attitude is likely to be positive. Determine to reinforce this. If the number of negative traits is greater than the positive, then your overall attitude is likely to be negative. If this is the case, avoid being defensive, and work out a plan to change it. If there are an even number of positives and negatives, then you may be well-balanced for now, but you could work on trying to get more positives. Write out a plan below for how you can attain and maintain a very positive and empowering attitude.

   _____

   _____

   _____

   _____

2. Work on displaying dignity and treating others with dignity by doing or saying only what is respectful, productive, and endearing. Whenever you are addressing someone or faced with any situation, bear in mind to do so with as much dignity as can be mustered. Write out below the elements of what you consider to be dignifying speech and behavior. Ask a coach, friend, or partner to read through this and assess how suitable it is.

   _____

   _____

   _____

   _____

   _____

3. A. Now you need to find out about the settings of your internal expectations thermostat. Start with a personal audit by listing below your own personal abilities, opportunities, strengths, and weaknesses.

Abilities: _____

_____

_____

Opportunities: _____

_____

_____

Strengths: _____

_____

_____

Weaknessess: _____

_____

_____

Based on the above, and in line with your vision or goals, write out a plan below on how you can improve on your abilities, strengths, and opportunities as much as possible while working on reducing your weaknesses.

_____

_____

_____

_____

_____

_____

_____

_____

B. Next, to know your general expectations, define clearly what you expect out of life or from any particular situation, vision, or goal.

_____

_____

_____

_____

_____

_____

_____

Now match below what you have written out as your expectations above with your abilities, strengths, and opportunities, which you identified earlier.

_____

_____

_____

_____

_____

_____

_____

From the exercise above, now consider the following:
- If your expectations and opportunities match your abilities or are slightly higher, then you may be well-balanced in the setting of your expectation thermostat, or you probably have even challenged yourself slightly.
- If your expectations are considerably higher than your abilities, then check again to find out if you have set unrealistic expectations or if you have underrated your abilities and opportunities.
- If your expectations fall far below your abilities or opportunities, then you may have set your expectation thermostat too low, or you have overrated your abilities or opportunities and need to cross-check them all again.

Once you have done your cross-checks, reset your expectation thermostat to the realistic level and write it out below.

_____

_____

_____

_____

_____

_____

Next work to keep focusing your mind on these expectations while using your personal abilities to maximize your opportunities and minimize your identified weaknesses.

4. Now focus on developing an action orientation. First, write below your favorite reasons for not always taking action toward your goals at any point in time.

_____

_____

_____

_____

This is your procrastination list, and in here are all the usual excuses preventing you from reaching your goal. Now find a coach, mentor, or friend. Take each reason listed above, and explain to yourself and someone who can hold you accountable why that reason is strong enough for you not to take action toward your goal. The aim here is to get you to really try to justify why you cannot take action. For the ones you cannot really justify, cross them off the list, and whenever you try to use them as excuses again, remember they are not valid. For the ones you are able to justify, these may be based on well-ingrained limiting beliefs, and you will need to work to get rid of limiting beliefs. Do this by drawing up a positive and empowering affirmation statement below that directly opposes each of your limiting beliefs causing you to procrastinate.

5. You spend the most amount of time with yourself. Therefore, you need to keep up self-motivation. You do this using an emotional anchor, which could be someone, something, or a belief you cherish and love dearly. For motivation, you can also use pain fuel or success fuel, which, respectively, are situations that have given you heartache you never want to experience again or situations that have given you joy you want to have again. You can also get motivation from things that you are grateful for. So write out below what qualifies as your own emotional anchors, pain fuel, success fuel, and things to be grateful for.

Emotional Anchors: _____

_____

Pain Fuel: _____

_____

Success Fuel: _____

_____

Gratefulness: _____

_____

Keep this list and use it as one of those tools which can help to keep you motivated.

6. It is important that you relax and enjoy yourself with decent activities. Relaxation will help to take your mind off the pressures of conducting business in a tough terrain and will also give your brain some needed rest. You will come back refreshed, energized, and with new perspectives to overcome your challenges and achieve success. Write below the activities you love to do, and then schedule a time beside each activity for when you plan to do it.

_____

_____

_____

_____

_____

Share your plans with a friend who can encourage you to stick with your plans. Then also commit to doing everything you can to take these times to relax and replenish your energy and motivation. Even jungle can wait a bit for you to go away and have some fun, so do it.

Chapter Ten Reflections on Attitude

Note here your personal reflections from the exercises in this chapter. Also prepare a to-do list of tasks or steps you will take daily to implement the exercises.

_____

_____

_____

_____

_____

_____

_____

_____

_____

_____

_____

_____

_____

_____

_____

_____

_____

_____

_____

Conclusion

After working through these exercises, you should by now have become quite familiar with some of the Junglepreneur concepts and frameworks. It is also believed that you have started applying them to your business and circumstances already. If this is the case, then there is no doubt whatsoever that you will achieve faster and more effective results by using this workbook. After completing this workbook, it is suggested that the next step you should take is to sign up for follow-up consulting or coaching sessions with Junglepreneur consulting services. The follow-up consulting or coaching sessions will empower you and help address any business issues you need to focus on. They can also be personal mentoring or accountability sessions to help keep you on track for the goals you have set. The sessions can also help you to walk through the different Junglepreneur frameworks on a deeper level and to then identify and implement the specific ones that are suited for your needs. During these guided sessions, you can also develop a Junglepreneur Terrain Action Plan (TAP), which is your very own roadmap for taming your terrain. Additionally, you can also get premium access to more advanced tools, such as the Junglepreneur RETINA framework for thinking outside the box, among others. If eligible, you can also qualify to be invited to the highly enabling Junglepreneur Mastermind sessions. To discuss further on the consulting or coaching sessions or to make a booking, please get in touch through www.junglepreneur.com. I wish you great success in your journey; may the terrain favor you.

David Oludotun Fasanya

ACKNOWLEDGEMENTS

Just like my first book, Way of the Junglepreneur, it also took a whole town to get this workbook ready. So I am very grateful to God, my family, friends, editors, graphic designers, production managers and associates for making this publication possible.

Junglepreneur Workbook Personal Notes

_____

_____

_____

_____

_____

_____

_____

_____

_____

_____

_____

_____

_____

_____

_____

_____